HOW TO BECOME A

BUSINESS TO BUSINESS DEBT NEGOTIATOR

In as little as 7 Days…
With Little or No Capital…
Make big money FAST…
Thrive in Any Economy

J. LANCASTER

DISCLAIMER

This book is sold for informational purposes only to provide information regarding how to start a Business to Business Debt Negotiation company.

The author and publisher make no warranties or representations with respect to the accuracy, applicability, fitness, or completeness of the contents of this program. An attempt has been made to provide accurate information on the subject matter covered and the author and publisher have used their best efforts in preparing this program.

We shall have no liability or responsibility to anyone with respect to contracts negotiations or agreements that may result from information in this book, or for any loss or damage caused or alleged to have been caused directly or indirectly by such information. The author and publisher shall in no event be held liable for any loss or other damages, including but not limited to special, incidental, consequential, or other damages.

We are not attorneys. We are not engaged in the rendering of legal advice. If legal advice is required, the assistance of a competent, qualified legal professional should be sought. We disclaim any loss, either directly, or indirectly, as a consequence of applying the information presented herein.

This book may not be reproduced in any form, in whole or part, without the express written consent of the publisher.

A BRIEF DESCRIPTION OF BUSINESS TO BUSINESS DEBT NEGOTIATION

The profession of Business and Debt Negotiation is a huge industry. Although this is not a new concept, <u>this Business is needed now more than ever!</u> The beauty of this business is it's LONGEVITY; twenty years from now, there will be businesses that need to resolve their debts. This business is not dependant on interest rates, stock markets, or any outside influence which may affect may other businesses.

You purchased this book because you want to grow your own business and not rely on others for your security. KNOW that Debt Negotiation is a REAL BUSINESS. This is not an MLM, or GET QUICK FAST Scheme. There are no products to sell. Debt Negotiation is a Professional Service you offer. The type of Debt Negotiation this book covers is **BUSINESS TO BUSINESS!**

 This is your own business that you build (quickly) and work for many years. Eventually, you can hire people to work for you. The possibilities and compensation are infinite!
You will learn how to help others and become very financially successful doing so!

In our present economic environment, there are hundreds of thousands of unresolved **Business** disputes all over everywhere.   After enormous stress, aggravation, and wasted time trying to collect on a debt, most parties feel that their only option is to take legal action to at least try to recoup some of the money owed to them. Who can blame them?

Most of us dread going through the legal system. Can you spell S T R E SS? We've accepted that going this route is expensive, emotionally draining, and it takes what seems like forever.

Hum…seems the situation hasn't changed much from what they were experiencing before deciding to get involved with the Legal System.. Now it is just going to cost them a lot of money in Legal fees. Not much has changed, has it?   There must be a better way!

This is where you come in..

EVERYONE INVOLVED BENEFITS FROM YOUR SERVICE

YOU ARE THE ALTERNATIVE TO THE LEGAL SYSTEM

All parties benefit!!!!!

Your Client the Debtor, the Company he owes money to, and <u>you</u> for your services rendered in resolving their dispute to everyone's satisfaction.

HOW THE *DEBTOR* (YOUR CLIENT) BENEFITS

1. You work with your Client on a NO RESULT-NO FEE basis. If nothing comes about, he owes you nothing. He has nothing to lose.

2. Resolution is usually achieved in less than a week.

3. You are reducing the stress between the parties involved. At this point, they are too emotionally involved to resolve much of anything!

4. You are the Alternative to the Court System! You are saving your Client Court Fees, filing fees, legal fees – which he would have to pay whether he wins or not! Time in Court takes away from time making money! Court appearances are costly and very time consuming!

5. **His business survives – he can move ahead.** His reputation is back on track. He may even be able to conduct business with the Creditor again, should it be beneficial to both parties.

HOW THE CREDITOR (Business owed the money) BENEFITS:

1. **He gets paid.**

2. He is not dragged through the court system, only to get a judgment which he has to try to collect on anyway.

3. **He gets paid**

HOW YOU BENEFIT:

1. **You get paid first. YOU GET PAID WELL.** You never wait for your money. Most of the time, it will take you a few days to a week to resolve a debt situation.

2. You've gained your Client's trust and he will refer you to others, and probably use you again himself.

3. The Company, who finally got paid because of your efforts, also refers your services to others and knows that they can contact you to resolve debt situations they may have themselves. . You are always fair and professional to all parties involved – never burn your bridges.

4. You are building a network of clients every time you successfully negotiate a debt situation. You are the "go-to guy" (or gal!).

This is how you build your business!

"The person who makes a success of living is the one who sees his goal steadily and aims for it unswervingly. That is dedication"

Cecil B. DeMille)1881-1959) American Filmmaker

DO I HAVE WHAT IT TAKES TO DO THIS?

"All glory comes from daring to begin." Anonymous

Think about this- you negotiate every single day in your life without even realizing it! You negotiate with teachers, your kids, your spouse, your co-workers, over the phone or in person with companies you do business with.

Here's what you need to make this business work
(It is not about much education you have)

- *You need common sense*

- *You need to be able to communicate in a clear and effective manner.*

- *You need to be taken seriously as one who possesses the <u>knowledge</u> and <u>ability</u> to resolve problems.*

- *You need determination. You see results quickly, there is always a learning curve with a new project -– you will make mistakes and learn from them.*

- *You need to be the kind of person who gets satisfaction from helping others with their problems. Tell me that you haven't had "sit downs" with friends and families and helped guide them through difficult times..*

- *You need to be reliable*

	You also need to enjoy making lots of money.

QUESTIONS YOU MAY HAVE BEFORE READING THIS BOOK

Q. How can I describe what I am doing?

A. You are a Business to Business **Debt Negotiator.** You can also refer to your self as an *"Arbitrator".*

An Arbitrator "achieves settlement and brings the process to terms"
A Negotiator "gets past a hurdle and brings conclusion to a matter"

Q. Who am I representing?

You are always and only representing the Debtor (not the Creditor)

Q. I don't have any legal experience. Can I still do this?

A. First and foremost never "play lawyer". *You never give a legal opinion.* You are a **Negotiator**, not an Attorney. You will learn all you need to know through this book to become a successful Negotiator.

Q. Do I need a license to do this?

A. We don't know that you need a license to *provide a service* in your particular state. We suggest getting the regular Occupational Business License through your County. They run around $100 or so and you need to renew every year. Having a license also makes you appear more Professional and Credible.

Q. Is this business "portable"?

A. That's the beauty of this business. You can do it in your home town or start anywhere else. You are your own boss and if like most of us, work from your home office wherever that may be!

Q. Is it hard to find Clients?

  A. You will have all the business you need and we'll show you where to find it.

Q. How long should it take to see some income?

  A. Most Negotiations are resolved within the week. It depends on when you get started. Typically, we see an average debt resolution bring compensation in about 2 weeks from start to finish.

Q. How do I know how much to charge?

  A. *You receive a percentage of what you save the Debtor*, your client. You are negotiating on his behalf - always. The customary fee is 35% of the amount you saved him. Or, if you set up a Payment Plan for him with his Creditor, your compensation is 10% of the **Gross** amount. This is your business and you can set your fees as you see fit. These percentages are what works for us and are fair for the parties involved. We have never been questioned about our fees – so we feel that they are a good guide for you to follow.

Here are a couple of examples of Settlement Agreements and how much Earned Commission you would make:

ABC Builders owes Morris Lumber Company $15,000. Morris Lumber has agreed to accept $8,000 provided that payment is made within 72 hours. ABC Builders saved $7,000. Your fee is 35% of the $7,000 or $2,450.

✲✲✲✲

Melanie Fashions owes Stylish Handbag Company $24,000. You set up an extended payment plan for them over X- amount of years, beginning immediately. Your fee is 10% of the GROSS, or $2,400 payable immediately.

I'M READY TO LEARN! BRING IT ON!

You will be very well rounded in this field by the time you finish this book. Read it over and over again. You will learn:

- The psychology behind Negotiating – understanding both sides of the fence establishing a rapport with the Debtor.

- How to set up your business and get started.

- Where to find clients

- The type of cases to get involved in.

- Overcoming objections

- Receiving your payment

- Paperwork involved – understanding your agreements

    And much more!

Remember, this is your business. How well you do is determined by you and you alone. This book will give you the insight and information you need to be successful.

"Success or failure is caused more by mental attitude than by mental capacity".

Sir Walter Scott (1771-1832) Scottish novelist, poet

TABLE OF CONTENTS

FORMS

A little about the author

I started doing Business to Business Debt Negotiation about 15 years ago. I had just "escaped" from an abusive *marriage* where I was made to believe (and let myself buy into it) that I was worthless, incapable of making any decision, and had no purpose in life.

Prior to this *marriage*, I was strong, independent, and well liked. I allowed myself to turn into a ball of mush, and longed for the person I used to be, but felt "stuck" and just existed in that mess from day to day.

I had three kids one only 10 months old. This was about the time when the whole "OJ "Saga was taking place, and as I watched TV, I saw myself as the next "Nicole".

THAT WAS MY WAKE UP CALL… I had no family to help me, so I sold some items I had treasured, put a deposit on an apartment, enrolled my kids in a new school, lined up a job (took a job at a Daycare to get some immediate income) and filed Divorce Papers.

Over a short period of time, I achieved little "goals" and my confidence started to come back. I wanted more and needed to make more money, but also wanted to be able to spend time with my kids who really needed me. A friend of mine told me about how her career in "Business to Business Debt Negotiation" had flexible hours, was exciting and rewarding and best of all she was making great money! She convinced me that I could be just as successful pointing out that I had everything I needed right now to get started.
I was a good negotiator and planner and always had a good work ethic. She commented on that fact that my motivation to succeed and provide a comfortable life for myself and my kids was the force that could only lead to success. I was so ready.   We had coffee and I took

notes on what she was saying. This business just seemed to "make sense".

I had the basic concept, but had no specific "Guidelines" to follow; so I winged it. I took a lot of notes and formed my own plan based on common sense and the fact that a contract is only as good as the people who sign it.

I cut my work days at the Daycare down to 3 days and week and researched and worked with an "invincible desire" to make this very simple business pay off.

It did. People liked me. They seemed to feel comfortable and trusted me. I had been through so much myself and I could empathize with their situation. I *really* wanted to help them. After the first few small resolutions came through, I devoted every day to growing this business and taking on larger settlements.

At this point in my life, my children are grown one in High School, two married and doing well. I decided to share this business opportunity and help others discover just how rewarding and financially satisfying this Business is.

My kids remember the tough times and still tell me that they "respect me" for going on limb and taking the "Chance" for a better future- not wanting a "Mediocre Life".

"Never look down to the test the ground before taking your next step; only he who keeps his eye fixed on the far horizon will find his right road".

Dag Hammarskjold (1905-1961)
Swedish statesman, U.N. Secretary (1953-1961)

"Parley"

NOT JUST FOR PIRATES….

If you are a fan of the Pirates of the Caribbean Movies, with the infamous Captain Jack Sparrow, you will recall that on more than one occasion a "Parley" was called!

The term Parley (par leeh) is from the French verb, meaning "To Speak". The origin of this verb is somewhere between 1400-1450.

The definition is: "To hold a conference between "enemies" under a truce, to discuss terms, condition, options."

Unfortunately, when a Creditor is owed money from a Debtor, emotions run high and although no one is an "enemy", these two parties are in conflict with each other.
Therefore, *to parley* is to use one's talents to achieve a desired objective" – for us, a successful resolution of a debt between two business entities.

Negotiators have been resolving differences for centuries!

A VERY SIMPLE BUSINESS – HELP OTHERS AND HELP YOURSELF

This is a very simple business and could not be timelier in our current economic environment. More and more businesses are finding themselves in debt and are grasping to stay afloat.

A recession is a horrible thing – but as you know, sometimes what is a bad situation for one is an opportunity for another. If you happen to be in a position to buy Real Estate right now, you will get some fantastic deals. Your ability to invest in a property may be helping someone else unload what is a "sponge" to them, so they can move ahead. It's a win-win situation in most cases.

The same is true for a Business to Business Debt Negotiator . With Court costs so high, you are the *Alternative to the Legal System,* helping businesses stay afloat and keep their reputations. You are the problem solver.

You are about to study a business known as "Business to Business Debt Negotiation". You will be known as a Business Debt Negotiator, Business Debt Arbitrator, or a Business Debt Consultant. They all basically mean the same thing. You will provide a service to Businesses whereby you will negotiate payment with the Creditor on behalf of the Debtor (your client) with the goal of bringing a successful resolution to all parties on the debt owed.

Just about everything is negotiable. As stated previously, we negotiate every single day of our lives (we just don't realize it!) No matter what your role in life, Negotiating is a part of our life. Are you married or in a relationship? There you go – you're negotiating all the time! Got kids! Same thing! But you get the picture – this comes naturally.

Negotiating in a business environment is a process. You really need to understand that financial problems, especially in the last few years, have generated enormous anxiety for the parties involved. Our country is struggling with an enormous debt, and businesses are going under on a daily basis. Just look around in your own neighborhood.

We are talking BUSINESS in this manual, but on a personal level, we have all been through some tough financial situations where we would find it hard to sleep, relax, or even think straight. A person in this situation will find that they are reacting more to emotions when trying to negotiate a debt. They are dealing with the Creditor, who handed out his goods or services in good faith, and never got paid! So here we have two parties at odds with each other.

Maybe the Debtor had all good intentions but came upon hard times and poor choices – he is just "over it". The Creditor is tired of asking and waiting for his money, he is definitely "over it".

What if a third party (you) were to come into the picture without all the pent up emotions, willing to negotiate a satisfactory resolution for your client and the creditor as well? We can represent our client in a way that he may not be able to do for himself at this point. We represent him as sincere in wanting to resolve this on-going debt situation.

You are the calming force that will reach an agreement for the parties involved. *You are*, as stated earlier, *the alternative to the legal system.* You are getting the parties to work things out for themselves, honoring a mutually satisfactory agreement.

One of the qualities you need to possess if you want to be successful at this business is to *really care* about the parties at hand and understand the stress that they have been going through. Your Client (we will call him your Client – he is the Debtor – always) will need to have confidence in you. He'll be giving you sensitive information which needs to remain with you and only with you. Never, ever, share personal information about a Client with ANYONE. It will come back to haunt you..

Your Purpose is to keep the Debtor out of the court system. The court system is ridiculous. There are thousands upon thousands of business disputes – hard to believe but depending on what city you live in, the courts can make you wait years for a court date! Here we are, resolving disputes, making all parties satisfied, within a week or so of taking the case!

Don't let the size of this book fool you..We could have added pages and pages of "psycho-babble" telling you how important it is to be determined, motivated and persistent. How you need to set goals for yourself.

You know that. If you were not motivated to achieve financial success, work for yourself, and control your own future, you would not have searched or purchased this book in the first place!

So here is my advice to you to be successful in business and in life:

"If you're interested, you'll do what's convenient, if you're committed, you'll do whatever it takes"!

Be Committed. This is a REAL CAREER, not a MLM, not a Get Rich Quick Scheme. You need to work at it. That's it. Just do it and you will see your goals come to fruition in a very short time.

It should take you no more than 7 days, to set up your business, get your leads, and make contacts. Again, this is a simple business which requires common sense, compassion, and motivation.

You will need a computer, internet connection and a phone which most likely, you are already set up with. The only investment we suggest is that you apply for a Business License under the category of "Consultant". More on this later – so bottom line is if you have about $100 for a license, you are ready to rock and roll..

SETTING UP YOUR BUSINESS

Your office: You'll need a computer, printer, phone, and the ability to fax (not everything is emailed).

Business License: You will need a business license from city (county) you are doing business in. It is sometimes referred to as an "Occupational Business License". They generally run close to $100 and you need to renew them every year. Google your county's official website – you may be able to apply online in some cases. When choosing a category, you would be considered a "Consultant".

Business Cards: If you want to be taken seriously, don't print your business cards out on your computer. This is a career. Your card represents you. You don't need to spend a fortune.
You can get beautiful glossy cards online from www.vistaprint.com at ridiculously low prices. Wherever you decide to purchase your cards, make sure they look PROFESSIONAL.

Create a professional sounding name for your company- with a "legal flair" to it. Example: "Weller and Weller" or "Weller, Henderson and Smith."
Use your name in there, along with other names that sound "lofty".
Under the name, describe what you do: *Business to Business Debt Negotiation.*

What not to choose:
 "Dewey, Cheatham, and Howe just won't work!" Three Stooges, anyone? (lol).   Initials sound like an MLM (TMJ Associates). In most cases, your business card is handed to your prospective Clients first, before they ever talk to you. So let it look "strong, reliable, and stable".

Your Physical Address (If you choose to use one):

Never, ever use a PO Box. If you don't want to use your home address, go to a Postal place and get a mailbox. You'll have a street address, and your mailbox number can be called a "suite".

Email address: Set up a professional sounding email address. This will be used on your business cards and other materials. Google has Gmail, which not only is an excellent service and is also free. YOUR NAME@gmail.com.

Good Phone Messages: "Hello. You have reached the office of Milner, Jones and Kelly. We are with Clients right now and unable to take your call. Your call is important to and will be returned promptly. Please leave, your name, number, and a brief message. All calls are handled with the strictest confidence". Thank you".

Simple, to the point, professional.

Bank Account: Your fee will be presented to you in the way of a Cashier's Check. Stay Professional with your Client. If your Business name (on your cards, etc) is "Milner, Jones and Kelly", you should expect your Client to have your Cashier's Check made out in the same manner. Asking him to make it out to Johnny Milner looks unprofessional as if you are hiding something from your other partners (even if they are just names and not really people).

Bring your Business License to the Bank and open an account as a DBA. (doing business as) . Straight Business Accounts usually carry high fees.
A DBA account will read (let's pretend your name is Johnny Milner) "Johnny Milner DBA Milner, Jones, and Kelly." Ask your bank of

choice which way is the most cost effective and best for your business in the long run.

WEBSITE: A website will give you credibility and serves as a "Billboard" for your business however, it is not necessary to get one right away.

If you cannot afford to have a professional in the field put one together for you (we have found that they usually charge about $300 and up), you might consider checking out www.hyperstreet.com.

If you can cut and paste, you can choose from tons of templates and quickly and easily put up a site, which you can update and change as needed. You can also buy a domain name at the site. (around $10) A typical website with lots of features goes for around ($100). You renew each year.

Check out their website to obtain more precise information. They offer a generous free trial period so you can to set up a site and try it out (it is not published on the internet, of course) before buying. It is worth checking out!

FORMS: You have our permission to Copy the forms at the end of the book for your personal use. **These forms are basic and straightforward and *should* be recognized in any state. Remember: A Contract is only as good as the people who sign it. PUT THESE FORMS ON YOUR LETTERHEAD.** (*Except* for the Settlement Agreements- more about that later**)** The next section will tell you which forms you need to bring to your first meeting.

YOU WANT TO LOOK "SOLID" IN OUR APPEARANCE AND THE MATERIALS THAT REPRESENT YOU!

Keep your receipts from everything for tax time. We are not accountants but many business expenses are deductible.

YOUR FEES

You receive a percentage of what you save your client. Your fee is 35% of the amount saved. If an extended payment plan is set in place, you receive 10% of the **GROSS.**

Payment Plan Example

King Contracting owes Yellow Lumber $19,650
You set up an extended payment plan for 3 years where King Contracting pays Yellow Lumber $545.83 each month. Your fee is 10% of the gross or
$1,965 payable at the time of the agreement.

Your fee is always received when you set up the arrangements. Never extend credit to your Client for your fee.

Lump sum payment Example

Mako Surf Boards owes Mitchell Fiberglass Co. $34,200. Mitchell agrees to accept $16,000 with payment within 24 hours. You saved Mako $18,200.
Your fee is 35% of the savings which is $6,370.

Keep in mind that most cases are resolved within a week (mostly within a few days). It is up to you to be diligent and work fast to resolve these matters. From the examples above, you can see the kind of income you can make with this business.

WHICH CASES DO I ACCEPT?

You want cases that will resolve quickly. At the beginning, until you have a few resolutions under your belt and feel comfortable, we suggest you deal with debts between $15,000 and $50,000.

As with all new ventures, there is a learning curve. Allow about a month to be comfortable. There is no limit on the dollar amount of cases you can handle. You have to crawl before you walk!

The best types of debts to tackle at first are: Outstanding bills between Debtor and Creditor, Past due accounts, accounts in dispute. After a little experience take a look at delinquent leases, rents (lots of those these days) these may be in retail or office spaces or leases on rental machines and equipment.

WHICH BUSINESSES SHOULD I TARGET?

The construction industry, especially now with the housing crisis, would be a top one. There are disputes with Sub-contractors, Landscapers, Tile Installation, Flooring, Electricians.

The Automobile and Trucking industry are other good prospects. These are just a few examples to start with.

Stay away from: Franchises as they are too "deep" with corporate decision makers" and it will take forever to resolve a case.

Make it a point not to get involved with Consumer Disputes. Keep it Business to Business. Some disputes require legal knowledge such as bank or credit card disputes. Leave those alone. They will be more trouble than they are worth.

FINDING YOUR CLIENTS

- Your warm market

People you know, businesses you deal with all the time. **DON"T** ask them if **THEY** owe money and are in Debt with someone, give them your card and say "Maybe *you know someone* who could use my service. I'll work to get them a substantial debt reduction with their creditors and it's on a **NO RESULT-NO FEE BASIS**. I really appreciate it!"

They may be the ones with the debt situation. You have to have some diplomacy because it can be embarrassing, and it is confidential.   Don't be surprised when you get a call from this party seeking your help.

Also remember- when you are dealing with friends or acquaintances they will drill you with questions on how you do it, etc. Just say that it is "involved" and "Confidential" and that you would be glad to call the person, or ask that they have the person they know give you a call.

Don't make the mistake of discussing your Fees, How you conduct the business. This is all Confidential.

- Choose an industry you want to work with and focus on it.

- Contractors for example use tile and granite guys, flooring people, etc. Sometimes there is a cash-flow problem with the contractor and he doesn't pay the sub-contractors as promised. He may owe more than one person and be overwhelmed. Tell him that you can Negotiate on his behalf to get a substantial reduction in what he owes. And always that it is on a **NO RESULT-NO FEE BASIS**

- The Distributors of building materials sell to the installers. For example, you can Google "Granite Installers". They may owe money to a distributor. Most probably, they want to continue doing business with this distributor and are looking for a way to resolve their debt.

- Google "Online Newspapers (your state)"
  Go to the Public Notices Tabs. Tons of info there.

- Check out the "Intent to Incorporate" list. Send these businesses your info for future reference – a need will come up sooner or later. They may be in business a while and *have recently decided to incorporate and may have existing debt issues you can help them with.*

- Your Town's Local Business Association will have listings of all their members. These Associations are not expensive to join and are fantastic for networking at their monthly meetings.

- Create a presence on social network sites like Face Book and Twitter.

- Secretary of State Website for your State.
  You can find complete info, names, addresses, phone numbers, contacts, by searching the "Business Category" tab.

- The Better Business Bureau (BBB.org) for your area has a multitude of lists

- Join a Networking Group in your area. The group consists of many businesses but only one business of any type. This is a great place for referrals.

- Chamber of Commerce Members List

- Business Journal Newspapers list new businesses

- Place an ad on Craig's List. Find the Business Section, Jobs Needed, Jobs Wanted, etc. Place a classified ad .

Make it simple

"BUSINESS OWNERS – Past due Bills? We Can Negotiate a discount with your Creditors. NO RESULT-NO FEE." Add your phone number, email or website.

- Check the Internet and Google "Free Advertising". There are tons of networking sites blogs and forums. Yahoo Groups is one of the largest. Get your name out there! Make others aware that your Services are available and that they are on a **NO RESULTS-NO FEE BASIS!**

- If you decide to put up a website, get in touch with other businesses who may have contacts for you. Ask them to let you put up a banner or small ad on their site, which will link to yours. Give them a percentage of any business that comes your way from them.

  - Physically go out and visit a small industrial center or strip centers.

    Seeing an ACTUAL PERSON instead of an email or voice message has a big impact! Speak to the owner, ask him a few questions about his business, location, etc. **You are trying to get him to ask you what *your* business is.**

    If he doesn't ask, just tell him that you are new in the area and give him your card.

**Ask him to please pass it along should he know of anyone who may need your help** (Don't ask if he needs your help (tacky!) – use discretion, be a diplomat!)

Make sure you state that it is on a **NO RESULT - NO FEE BASIS** so they would have nothing to lose! Many times, you will get a call from this owner, because he is the one with the debt situation!

When going out on cold calls, it is best to dress _business casual._ I never carried a briefcase but just a few business cards in my pocket. Remember, it's a simple business. No need to look like a pushy salesperson.

- Email or send out the _**Prospecting Letter**_ at the end of this manual. Keep an Excel sheet of who you are contacting so you can track your responses.

- Companies like www.constantcontact.com, icontact.com, informz.com, to name a few, are email services the let you create colorful informative emails with a tracking system built right in! You can see how many of your emails were opened, at what times, and how many times they were viewed! This information will give you your "hot list" – after all, if someone viewed your email five times, they must have some interest, right? You pay a monthly fee based on how many emails you wish to send out each month. The fees start at something like $15/month- check out their website and see what you think!

If you set a goal for yourself on a weekly basis, you will be successful in no time at all. **Get your name and what you do out there!** Take 1 day a week for physically going out and leaving materials, 3 days for searching on the internet, sending emails, preparing letters, making phone calls and one day for the Courthouse. (info below)

When you can settle a case for one of your clients in say 48 hours – You are on his AMAZING LIST! You will see more from him and the referrals will start coming in! Most clients will bring at least 2-3 cases to you – theirs or referrals. People *talk* in business- they know other people who are having problems and will feel like a "hero" by getting them in touch with you.

REMEMBER- WHEN TALKING TO ANY BUSINESS OWNER DON'T INFER THAT <u>HE</u> NEEDS YOUR HELP. ALWAYS ASK THAT HE JUSTS PASSES ALONG YOUR INFORMATION TO SOMEONE WHO MAY BE ABLE TO USE YOUR SERVICE

A WORD ABOUT PROSPECTING FOR CLIENTS IN THE BEGINNING:

Prospecting, at the beginning is "Work" but it will pay off in the long run. Think about what your RESULTS will be.. Put in the effort, be intentional and focused, and in a short time you will have so many referrals you won't have much time to prospect!

USING THE COURTHOUSE FOR LEADS

Public records are just that, public and open for anyone. Many times you can find these records online, but your particular county may not have them online.

New filings, which are your leads, come in every day. Start out with the smaller cases in SMALL CLAIMS COURT (up to $15,000).

Ask the Clerk for a few files. Don't be surprised if they ask if you are an Attorney. These are public files and you have every right to look at them. Simply say that you are an "Arbitrator, doing some research" Most of your info will be at the front and the back of the file. You are only interested in the Business to Business Disputes. The Defendant is your CLIENT.

Use the Courthouse Info Sheet in the back of the book or create an Excel Sheet on your laptop to capture information. Courthouses have different systems; the majority showing a Case number, date, date the suit was filed, names of the parties, and the type of Case (Indebtedness, Breach of Contract, etc). Flip through the file and ascertain how complicated it may be. At first, look for disputes that the Creditor filed on his own without an attorney. Get the Defendants Name and Business – you will have to look up his phone info on the internet, as it probably will not be in the file.

These are disputes that the Plaintiff has filed. They need to be answered within 20-30 days. If there is no response from the Defendant in this time frame, a judgment can be filed against them, it will adversely affect their credit, and they will just lose by default. Your goal is to help the Debtor (Defendant) resolve this matter before it gets to court. It is a summons at this point.

Business Journals are published weekly, usually on a Friday. Ask the Clerk which Business journal has all the listings of the CIVIL CIRCUIT cases. Jot down info from the Journals. These are your leads.

Call your leads and only speak to the Defendant. If anyone but the Defendant answers the phone (ex: secretary, Receptionist) Never give the reason for your call. "It is in reference to a legal matter". If he is not in, ask that he calls you back. If you don't hear from him in a day or two, call back. Try early. Business owners usually get in earlier than employees. If he is not interested, that's fine. Wish him well and move on to the next lead.

YOUR CLIENT

Your Client owes a Debt that he has avoided paying for a long enough period of time that the Creditor has decided to take action to recoup money owed to him. Maybe the Creditor has hired an Attorney or gone to a Collection Agency. Maybe he has just *threatened to do* so if the Debtor doesn't come through with payment within a stated period of time, and then he will take legal action to collect.

What options does your Client have?

1. He can get an Attorney and go to court. They request substantial retainers – whether you win or lose you pay.

2. If he legitimately owes this debt, he will lose in court.

3. The Creditor will get a judgment against him and try to collect however he can. He can put a lien on your Client's house, car, bank account, etc.

4. Your Client's credit will show a judgment or lien or both.

POSITIVE OUTCOMES BY USING YOUR SERVICES

1. He can let you resolve the problem, no courts, on a NO RESULT-NO FEE basis.

2. He can satisfy his Creditor with what HE can afford

3. He can stretch out his debt over a period of time so that he is not financially "strapped"

4. He can resolve his debt, get back to business and if beneficial to both parties, resume a working relationship with the Creditor

IMPORTANT – SO WE'LL SAY IT AGAIN

If a summons has been filed against your Client, he needs to know that he only has 20-30 days to respond. If he does not respond within the granted frame, a judgment can be filed, his credit rating Damaged, and if he doesn't show up for court, he'll just lose by default.

It's really important to convey to him that there really is a **sense of urgency** in the matter.

CONTACTING YOUR CLIENT

Sometimes…You have to get past "The Gatekeeper"

Contact your prospective Client **by phone.**

Many times your call will be answered by the dreaded "Gatekeeper" (I hear the "Jaws" theme in my head when I talk about Gatekeepers!)

The "Gatekeeper" is usually the Client's assistant or may be the receptionist. They have been instructed to screen calls, and this is what they do!

They will interrogate you! What do you want? Who are you? And What is the purpose of your call? are questions they usually ask. **Do Not going into a any "story" and give information to the Gatekeeper!**

The best way to handle this is to say who you are, and the name of your company and then say, "It's regarding a financial matter that I know Mr. __ would consider confidential.. Can you tell him I'm on the line please.."

When you get Your Prospective Client on the Phone:

Tell him that you understand he has a dispute with "ABC Company" and that you can assist him in coming to a resolution. You explain your services to him: You represent him negotiating on his behalf before his dispute ever gets to the courthouse. You can reduce his payables by 40%-80%. Using your service eliminates the huge expenses created with the legal system. You also eliminate his stress and wasted time by having you handle the situation.

You are offering services on a **NO RESULT- NO FEE BASIS**. *He has nothing to lose* by having you negotiate for him, and *only everything to gain.*

REMEMBER- If you are a business being sued, you have to resolve the problem in order to stay in business. You can stall things just so long, and the longer you stall the less bargaining power you have.

SET UP YOUR APPOINTMENT

After he has agreed that you just may be the answer to his problem, set up an in-person meeting. When you set the appointment, do it in such a way that he understands you are going to be concise and to the point.

Set the appointment so it appears that you will be taking only 15 minutes of his time. Example: "I can do 9:15 tomorrow morning, or 3:45 Tuesday – which is best for you? I'll come by your office".

Give him the choice. Once you agree on a time and place, say

"Please be sure any partners or other decision makers involved are at the meeting so we are all on the same page".

THIS IS VERY IMPORTANT.

MAKE SURE YOU KNOW WHO THE DECISION MAKERS ARE – IT COULD BE JUST HIM, OR HIM AND HIS WIFE OR PARTNERS. YOU DON'T NEED ANY SURPRISES!

WHAT YOUR CLIENT NEEDS TO BRING TO YOUR MEETING

- **COPIES** of his paper work involving the debt he owes. Invoices, information on the Creditor (name, address, phone, email, etc) any Statements showing the debt and payments that he attempted to make, etc. Whatever he needs to create a clear picture of what is going on between him and the Creditor.

- **Make sure he brings you about 6 sheets of his letterhead.**(explanation to follow)

- **He will also need to bring a Retainer** which is fully refundable. You work on a NO RESULTS-NO FEE basis. (More on Retainers as you read on)

MEETING YOUR CLIENT IN PERSON

To consult- means to deliberate, to discuss

Your appointment is set. NEVER BE LATE.

If you are meeting at his office, be very observant. Is it in a decent area, nice cars in the lot? Any employees? He may be a sole proprietor and that is fine. Do you see inventory?   Think of yourself as "a profiler"…you are mentally pre-qualifying him.

Be sure to have the "Client Info Sheet, "Power of Attorney / Retainer" forms. All forms are in the back of this book. Be prepared to take notes.

Explain your services – **Make it simple**. Explain that you will negotiate a substantial reduction in his debt with the Creditor. If that is not feasible, you will set up an extended payment plan for him. Check out how much he owes and how long he has owed it. Don't promise anything- you haven't spoken to the Creditor yet! You are there to build his trust and create a rapport with him in person. Go over the paperwork he brought.

Make it crystal clear that it is a **NO RESULTS-NO FEE** deal. He has nothing to lose. You get the results, he pays. No results, he owes you nothing. This is why you want to pre-qualify the Client. You are planning on getting results – and your fee is part of the deal!

HE NEEDS TO KNOW YOUR FEE UPFRONT

Explain that your fee is 35% of the savings to him if you Negotiate a debt reduction, or your fee is 10% of the Gross amount owed if you Negotiate a payment plan. Give him an example of each scenario.

(Use any of the scenarios in this book if you wish...they are just examples to paint a clear picture of how the fee is based..)

NOW IS THE TIME TO DETERMINE IF YOUR PROPECTIVE CLIENT CAN ACTUALLY PAY YOU AND HIS SETTLED DEBT -OR - IF HE HAS ALL *GOOD INTENTIONS* BUT NO FUNDS TO DO IT!

Use your "Client Info Sheet" as a Guide – then take notes as the conversation ensues.

Does your Client have the funds to settle the case with a Debt Reduction?
Show him on paper where you feel the bottom dollar will be. How much money does he have to work with to resolve this debt in a settlement?

If he has most of the money, but needs to "come up" with more, where is he planning to get it from, and what exact date will he have it by.

If it seems that his cash-flow is not adequate for payment reduction settlement, **pursue the payment plan instead.**

Tell him that you understand his situation and it is not unusual. Sometimes you just don't have the cash-flow to pay off the debt in one lump, even with a substantial reduction. Tell him that an **Extended Payment Plan** works very well and it could be for one, three, or five years and will take the pressure off.

How much can he afford in payments each month? A monthly payment to the Creditor should be 2-5% of the debt. So, as an example, if he owes $12,000 he should expect to have a monthly payment of between $250-$600 a month. **Make sure that there is cash to pay your fee (10% of the Gross in this case)**

If he doesn't have the funds, you need to walk away

PS- If you explained yourself well enough on the phone before your meeting, and went over his debt amount, and asked if a reduction in debt were possible to satisfy all parties, would that work for him…this should not happen.

QUESTIONS YOUR CLIENT MAY ASK YOU...

"I'd like some references from your past Clients"

Just as an example and this will happen often, you are speaking to prospective client explaining your service to him. He will ask for references from other people who have used your services. Makes sense. BUT- you have to respect your client's privacy at all times, past and present.

The right thing to say is "we treat our clients business in a strictly confidential manner. Just as you would not want me to give your name to my next prospective client, I would be violating a confidence and can't do that ". This type of statement produces trust.

After you have a few successes, ask for *written permission* from some satisfied clients to give their contact information out. Not everyone wants the world to know they had money problems, especially in business. However, some people will be glad to share that you helped them out in a tough situation and won't mind at all.

Always get the permission in writing. If you use that Debtor's name a few times, and he gives keeps giving you a stellar recommendation, show your appreciation now and then with a gift card to a local restaurant. It doesn't have to be much, but this gesture will show your gratitude and you know what they say: the more you give, the more you get!

"Are you an Attorney?"

No. **We negotiate**, attorneys litigate. Never give a legal opinion.

"Are you a Collection Agency?"

No. Collection agencies work for the Creditor. There fees are based on percentages typically receiving 40-50% of what they collect. Have you ever dealt with a Collection Agency? Their tactics are demeaning, intimidating, and many times down right rude.

We are the opposite side of the coin. We don't alienate the you and the Creditor; a mutual need may arise in the future where you may both benefit from working together. We again, work for you, the Debtor. We receive a percentage of what we save you, or in the case of our setting up an extended payment plan, we receive a percentage of the gross.

"Maybe I can just do this myself"

If you feel you can, then do it. If you believe you can get a 40-80% reduction on your debt why haven't you done so already?

"I have an Attorney, I'm sure he can Handle this for me"

He can – but will be he able to get you a debt reduction? We Negotiate without getting involved with the court system. Our fees are based on results – does *your Attorney work on a NO RESULTS – NO FEE basis?*

"Sounds OK- I might be interested- can you email me something or send me something in the mail?"

I can do that – but seriously – a brochure can't solve your problem. Just take 15 minutes to meet with me at your office, and I'll go over specific details of how we can help you. There's no cost. If we can't get a reduced settlement that satisfies you, you pay nothing. You have nothing to lose, but a lot to gain. I have a few minutes tomorrow at 3:15 if that works for you".

"Once this is resolved, I really want to do business with this Creditor again – do you think that's possible?"

If you both had a good working relationship before this debt came into play, that should not be a problem. Don't be insulted if your business is welcome but on a COD basis for a while, that's usually how Creditors will conduct business with you for a while, until trust is built up again.

ACCEPTING THE CASE
AND
SIGNING THE LIMITED POWER OF ATTORNEY/RETAINER AGREEMENT

He is ready and commits to your service. . Take out your **Power of Attorney/Retainer Agreement.**

The **LIMITED POWER OF ATTORNEY** allows you to speak for your client and represent his interests to the Creditor. **THE RETAINER SECTION** represents commitment. Depending on the size of the case, you should get between $100 -$500. This solidifies the deal and lets you see that the Debtor is sincere in getting this resolved.

Fill out the amount of Retainer on the POWER OF ATTORNEY FORM. This shows him that the amount will be deducted from your fee when a resolution is met or REFUNDED IN FULL if a satisfactory resolution is not met.

ALL THE DECISION MAKERS INVOLVED WITH YOUR CLIENT MUST SIGN THESE FORMS!

CONTACTING THE CREDITOR

Here is where you will learn if you will be dealing directly with the Creditor, his Attorney or Legal Representative, or a Collection Agency.

(Many times this information is listed in the Courthouse Leads.)

Be sure to do your due diligence on the Creditor's situation. If this is a Courthouse Case, you have some information from the case file. Otherwise you should have sufficient background info from your Client.

Make sure that you are speaking to the "Person with the Power" to work with you. You will have a name either from the courthouse leads or your client; should a secretary try to take control, politely ask for the proper party.

Once again, if "The Gatekeeper" insists on getting information from you regarding your call before connecting you to the Creditor, just tell her that "it is a confidential legal matter that *Mr. Creditor* is aware of.

If she still will not put you through, ask what may be a better time or method to get in touch with the Creditor. Be firm, but polite.

OPENING THE CONVERSATION DIRECTLY WITH THE CREDITOR

"Good morning. This is John Milner of Milner, Jones and Kelly. I'm calling regarding your account with (Debtor's Company)."

"Good Morning. This is John Milner of Milner, Jones and Kelly. We've been retained to represent (Debtor). He sincerely wants to resolve this debt. Do you have a few minutes to go over this account"?

"Good Morning. (Introduce yourself). We have been retained to represent (Debtor) with regard to the Debt he owes you. We've been in touch with his other Creditors also, and advised them of his situation and motivation to come to a Settlement Agreement. They've all been very responsive, and we hope you will hear us out as well."

The Creditor may have "an attitude", be rude, be apprehensive, or just sort of surprised to get a call of this nature. Understand, that the Creditor just wants to get paid, and it has probably been a while, maybe close to a year, and he hasn't received anything. So you need to be understanding but in control of the conversation.

Let him know that you have been **retained by the Debtor** and that you are representing the debtor in an effort to Negotiate his debt on his behalf.

Remember all the objections/questions we went over – some of those will be asked here. If he's angry, that's understandable so empathize with him. You understand the situation, and want to settle the matter. Remind him that you are THE ALTERNATIVE TO THE COURT SYSTEM, and it is worth
a shot to try coming to an agreement this way, rather than everyone spending more time, money, and aggravation with the courts.

Here are a few bits of info you can use in your conversation with the Creditor:

"My Client is having a tough time financially and is working hard to keep afloat."

"Our Company is working to reconstruct his debts and get him on the right track again."

"We've been in touch with his other Creditors and they have been very understanding, and hopefully you will be too. We want to come to a resolution that will satisfy all involved."

Be a good listener, he'll probably want to vent. Explain that your Client is **motivated to settle this debt with him** and **your goal** is to have a settlement with a Cashier's Check (or payment plan) in his hands within 48 hours. (You already pre-qualified your Client, so you know what you are offering to the Creditor – either a lump settlement or payment plan)

Tell him that you know this action has just been sprung on him during this phone call, and that you will put the offer in the mail, or email it to him, so he can read it over.

You don't want to put pressure on the Creditor to accept this offer at first glance. He needs some time to analyze the offer and weigh his option of taking the offer – or not accepting and going to court.

Call him in 2 days as promised (suggestion: initial call on a Tuesday, follow up on a Thursday if possible to avoid the weekend lull...)

If he is not very happy with the offer presented, you still need to be understanding. Here are a few responses to his objections:

1. "I know what you're saying and I agree, but realistically, You've been trying to collect this money for a while now, right? Wouldn't it be better to just get this case resolved, and move on? I mean, who wants to deal with the whole court scenario? I can arrange to have a Cashier's Check to you immediately, and we can all just move ahead.

2. Do you really want to deal with the hassles of taking him to court? . It may take years, and will end up being more expensive and stressful to say the least. At the end of the day you'll obtain a judgment and have to chase him to get it. Why not resolve this now?"

HE WANTS TO NEGOTIATE BUT DOESN'T THINK THE REDUCTION IS FAIR.

He has the right to feel that way. Tell him that you will go back to your Client go back to your Client and see what other options are available and you'll get back to him in a couple of days.

It is like making an offer on a house; you go back and forth a few times and then come to an agreement. You're a Negotiator, this is what you do!

THE CREDITOR HAS AN ATTORNEY/LEGAL REPRESENTATIVE HANDLING IT

There are just a few things that are different in these situations and we will go over them in this next section:

Now you are dealing with a "Middle Man'- the Legal Representative will take your offer and present it to *his* Client, the Creditor.

You need to be extremely professional and not intimidated if asked if you are a lawyer or some other legal-type entity. Simply state that Attorneys litigate, you Negotiate. You are the Third Party intervening to settle the debt to everyone's satisfaction.
(They may even ask you about your fees! Just tell that that you "work on a percentage".)

When you make a Settlement offer, obviously, you know the most that your Client can afford to pay – so make sure that you stay in your boundaries. Allow room to negotiate, you'll go back and forth on this.
They'll need some time to review your offer. Start with a low offer: Your first offer should be about 10-20% of the debt.

Attorneys deal with settlements that are pennies on the dollar, so this is not new to them. You can go up from there – but obviously just to the point that you know your Client can afford. You are Negotiating, this is what you do.

THE CREDITOR HAS A COLLECTION AGENCY HANDLING IT

Collection Agencies are paid by receiving a percentage of *what they collect.* So, they want to collect as much as they can.

If you have ever dealt with collection people, they may be pleasant at first, but most try to be intimidating and often times nasty. It is the nature of their business. They deal with deadbeats, people who *just don't want to pay and they usually are chasing them down!* Your Client is **available** and **wants to pay.**

Understand, they will probably have an attitude with you because you are telling them "they have not done their job". Their job is to collect a debt, and you come into the picture collecting the debt. They have not been successful in their attempts to collect this debt. However, some money is better than no money and they will come around to a settlement so they can close their books on this particular case and move on.

Here are a few examples for opening the conversation:

"Hello, this is John Milner with ____. I'm calling regarding (Debtor) and the debt he owes to (Crditor). We've been working on a plan with our Client to get his debts resolved and are making this one time offer to all his Creditors; we will honor agreements with each Creditor in the order that we receive them."

"Times have been tough for so many of us recently, and (Mr. Debtor) anxious to resolve this matter and move ahead"

"You're are aware that my Client is going through some very hard times financially, and is making the effort to resolve his debts. The other Creditors we've contacted have been understanding and appreciate his effort to resolve these debts."

"My Client is trying hard to stay above water and keep his business. The last thing he wants to do is file bankruptcy – so we hope you will work with us to resolve this matter".

YOUR FIRST OFFER SHOULD BE 10-20% OF THE DEBT. YOU CAN GO UP FROM THERE, BUT YOU NEED TO ALWAYS DO THE VERY BEST FOR YOUR CLIENT.

"Here is what we can do, and we'll have a Cashier's Check to you within the next 48 hours. It's probably less that you were expecting, but please consider it. We can resolve this matter for $____ as payment in full"

"Under the circumstances, the best we can do is $____ as payment in full. We can get a Cashier's Check to you in the 48 hours."

DON'T MAKE THE OFFER AND STOP TALKING!! CONTINUE SPEAKING!

"Please consider our offer; we have many more Creditors to settle with. It's the best we can do under the circumstances"

THE COLLECTOR WILL SPEAK AND EITHER BE RESPONSIVE TO YOUR OFFER, INSULTED BY THE OFFER, OR NASTY.

Your Response:

"I know you haven't seen any results with him so far. I can arrange for a Cashier's Check to be in your hands within 48 hours" – Do you really think you can do better in court?"

"I've talked with him for hours, and this is the best he can do. You can take him to court, get a judgment against him, and chase him for who knows how long to collect on it, if you actually ever do.

YOU MIGHT HAVE TO NEGOTIATE AGAIN. OK. THIS IS WHAT YOU DO, BUT NOW YOU SEE THAT THEY ARE WILLING TO COOPERATE WITH A SETTLEMENT AGREEMENT, THIS IS WHY YOU MUST START LOW!

Collection agencies tend to ask for post dated checks. This is **not good** for your Client. You Negotiate: *One payment of a reduced amount* or *a payment plan*. **That's it.** No post dated checks.

Whether you are dealing with the Legal Representative or a Collections Agency, once the Agreement is made, follow the same procedures that are outlined under **"DEALING WITH THE CREDITOR DIRECTLY"**

A RESOLUTION IS REACHED

When a resolution is reached, the Creditor receives

(2) Completed Settlement Agreement Forms. (One will be for him and one for your Client).

THE SETTLEMENT AGREEMENT MUST BE ON YOUR CLIENT'S LETTERHEAD. (Remember- you obtained a few sheets of your Client's letterhead at your first meeting)
This must be signed and returned to <u>you</u> by the Creditor.

Never let the Creditor bypass you and go straight to the Debtor with this.

Ink signature. He cannot fax or email it back!
MAKE THIS PERFECTLY CLEAR TO THE CREDITOR.

If the Creditor is local, make arrangements to have the signed Settlement Agreement picked up. Courier services really don't charge much to pick up and deliver it is very professional and fast. The local courier we use will pick up our envelope and deliver it within 3 hours. They charge $35 for this service. We include a pre-paid envelope for the Creditor to return the Settlement Agreement to us. By doing this, it makes it hassle-free for the Creditor to return it in a prompt manner.

If the Creditor is out of town, overnight it to him, and put a pre-paid overnight envelope in the package for him to use.

It may cost you a few dollars to use a Courier Service or Overnight Mail. Usually postage and mailings, etc are deductible at tax time, so save all receipts.

By expediting the "Signing/Delivery" process, you are bringing yourself closer to PAY DAY. You get paid WELL, so it will be worth laying out a few dollars to get this done!

TIME TO FINALIZE AND GET PAID!

Set up an Appointment with your Client to Sign and Finalize the Agreement

Your Client is aware of the resolution amount, and knows how much your fee is.

Reiterate to him that he must have both Checks with him at your meeting: Your comission check minus the Retainer Fee, and either the Lump Sum Payment or First Extended Plan Payment for the Creditor.

Now that you have the Creditor's signed Agreements, it is time for your Client to sign the 2 agreements (ink signature).

Take back and hold the 2 Agreements.

Make sure he understands his new obligation to the Creditor.

Before handing over signed and completed copies of the Settlement Agreement to your Client, you are to receive payment. Have your Client sign the "Settlement Acceptance" form and collect your fee.

Once you are paid, give your Client his agreement. Send the Creditor's agreement to the Creditor via Certified/Return Receipt Requested mail with his Cashier's Check enclosed.

Give the Creditor a call and thank him and let him know that you have sent his signed copy of the Agreement and his Cashier's Check to him Certified Mail/RRR, so he can be "on the lookout" for it.

Courthouse leads – information sheets

Case#:_____ Date Recorded:_____

Date of Filing:_____ Amount:_____

PLAINTIFF:_____

Address:_____

Phone:_____ Email:_____

DEFENDANT:_____

Individual's Name:_____

Home Address:_____

Bus. Address:_____

Phone:_____ Email:_____

Type of Case:_____

Comments:_____

Case#:_____ Date Recorded:_____

Date of Filing:_____ Amount:_____

PLAINTIFF:_____

Address:_____

Phone:_____ Email:_____

DEFENDANT:_____

Individual's Name:_____

Home Address:_____

Bus. Address:_____

Phone:_____ Email:_____

Type of Case:_____

Comments:_____

Case#:_____ Date Recorded:_____

Date of Filing:_____ Amount:_____

PLAINTIFF:_____

Address:_____

Phone:_____ Email:_____

DEFENDANT:_____

Individual's Name:_____

Home Address:_____

Bus. Address:_____

Phone:_____ Email:_____

Type of Case:_____

Comments::

INFO ON YOUR CLIENT

Appointment: _____ Location:_____ Confirm Appt: Phone and Email
_____

                 Origin of Lead: Courthouse___ Referral___ Other_____

1. What type of business? What exactly do they do? How long have they been in business?

   _____

2. How do they generate income? Internet Sales? ____ COD? ____Send out invoices?____

3. What is the typical grace period offered before the debt is considered late? 30 days? 60 days?

4. What is their cash flow situation? Positive, Negative?

5. Are they expecting any substantial Accounts Receivable payments?

6. Are they disputing one debt or do they have several?

7. Are there a number of disputes (money owed) from one Creditor in particular, or a number of outstanding accounts with varying creditors?

WHO:_____ Amount Owed?_____ How long has amount been delinquent?___   Methods used to try to collect :_____
WHO:_____ Amount Owed?_____ How long has amount been delinquent?___   Methods used to try to collect :_____

8. Where will the funds come from to settle the debt and Pay Earned Commission Fee?

   Can they sell property, inventory to obtain funds to settle the debt?

9. How many employees do they have?_____

10. Are they able to meet Payroll? _____

11. Are they considering Bankruptcy? __ Chapter?____

12. Legal Advisor?_____ Collection Agency_____

LIMITED POWER OF ATTORNEY / RETAINER AGREEMENT

TO ALL PERSONS, be it known that I, _____ of
_____ hereby make and grant a limited and specific
Power of Attorney to _____ of_____
And appoint and constitute said individual as my Attorney-In-Fact.

My named Attorney-In-Fact shall have full power and authority to undertake,
commit and perform only the following acts on my behalf.
Attorney-In-Fact agrees to act and perform in said fiduciary consistent with my best
interests in negotiating on by behalf with various Creditors/Plaintiffs reasonable
settlements of all claims owing.

Both parties agreement that this appointment does not create personal liability on
the part of _____ for any debts that the Debtor has incurred, and this
Agreement carries an obligation on behalf of the Debtor to honor all negotiated
settlements. _____is obligated to provide professional advice to effect the best
reasonable settlement.

Both parties agree and understand that this Agreement allows for a Retainer in the
amount of $____. This amount shall be fully credited against any Earned
Commissions, the amount being 35% of the SAVINGS TO YOU, our Client, or,
should an Extended Payment Plan be arranged, there will be a Fee of 10% of the
GROSS AMOUNT. The RETAINER IS FULLY REFUNDABLE IF NO
SETTLEMENT IS REACHED.

_____ OF _____ agrees to Negotiate on behalf
of_____ on a NO RESULTS-No FEE basis.

All Earned Commissions are due and must be paid upon Verification and
Acceptance of the Settlement Agreement. . This arrangement is not flexible, and
non-payment upon completion of transaction will automatically cancel the arranged
settlement with the Creditor and/or Representative. Should legal action become
necessary to enforce payment of Fee upon conclusion of case, the Client will be
responsible for legal cost.

Both parties agree that this Limited Power of Attorney may be severed at any time,
provided reasonable notice is given.

A Retainer Fee of $_____ (Teller's check/MO #_____ cash___) has been
received by _____ from_____ dated_____

_____   _____
            Sign   **Sign**

SETTLEMENT ACCEPTANCE

Claim Amount: $_____

RE: _____
        Debtor (Defendant)

VS: _____
        Creditor (Plaintiff)

_____ **I hereby accept the Negotiated Settlement.
Earned Commission Fee is attached per our Agreement/Limited Power of Attorney**

_____ **I am NOT accepting Negotiated Settlement.
I understand the Settlement negotiated on my behalf by _____
will be cancelled, per our Agreement/limited Power of Attorney and my Retainer Fee will be
reimbursed via Certified Mail within 3 business days of this signing.**

_____ **Date:_____**

_____ **Date:_____**

DEBT SETTLEMENT AGREEMENT (*lump sum payment*)

Agreement made on (date) between _____ of _____ (*Company name and address*) hereinafter referred to as Creditor, and _____ of _____ _____ (Company name and address) , hereinafter referred to as Debtor

In consideration of this agreement and the sum of _____ *Dollars (\$__)* to be paid to the Creditor by Debtor, Creditor agrees to release and forever discharge Debtor from all claims and demands arising out of the debt hereinafter described.

A.   Acknowledgement of Existing Obligation

The parties acknowledge that Debtor is at present in debt in the sum of ____Dollars (\$__) in connection with the following obligation: _____

1.   Agreement for Different Method of Payment

Debtor and Creditor desire, and they agree to provide for payment of the above-stated indebtedness in accordance with terms and provisions different from and in substitution of the terms and provisions of payment contained in the original contract described in Paragraph 1.

2.   Consideration/Method of Payment

In consideration of the mutual promises contained in this agreement, Debtor and Creditor agree as follows:

Debtor agrees to pay Creditor, and Creditor agrees to accept from Debtor in full satisfaction of the indebtedness describe in Paragraph 1 above, the sum of:
_____Dollars (\$_____) As follows:

Full payment by Cashier's Check   (Circle method)

(1) Sent Certified Mail/Return Receipt Requested within 24 hours of this signed agreement

(2) Hand delivered to the Creditor's place of business within 24 hours of this signed agreement

B. Default by Debtor

1.   Time is declared to be of the essence in this agreement and if the Debtor should fail to make the payment as provided in this agreement, the Creditor is released forever from his/her/its/obligation to accept from Debtor the lesser sum of _____Dollars (\$__) and shall have no further obligations under this agreement.

C. Satisfaction

On full payment by the Debtor to the Creditor of the payment provided in Paragraph 3 above, the original indebtedness of the Debtor to the Creditor as described in Paragraph 1 shall forever be cancelled and discharged.

_____(date)   _____(date)
Creditor   Debtor

_____   _____
Witness for Creditor   Witness for Debtor

DEBT SETTLEMENT AGREEMENT (*payment plan*)

Agreement made on (date) between _____ of _____ (*Company name and address*) hereinafter referred to as Creditor, and _____ of _____ _____(Company name and address), hereinafter referred to as Debtor

In consideration of this agreement and the sum of _____*Dollars (\$__)* to be paid to the Creditor by Debtor in the form of an **Extended Payment Plan**, Creditor agrees to release and forever discharge Debtor from all claims and demands arising out of the debt hereinafter described.

A.   Acknowledgment of Existing Obligation

The parties acknowledge that Debtor is at present in debt in the sum of ____Dollars (\$__) in connection with the following obligation: _____

1.   Agreement for Different Method of Payment

Debtor and Creditor desire, and they agree to provide for payment of the above-stated indebtedness in accordance with terms and provisions different from and in substitution of the terms and provisions of payment contained in the original contract described in Paragraph 1.

3. Consideration/Method of Payment

In consideration of the mutual promises contained in this agreement, Debtor and Creditor agree as follows:

Debtor agrees to pay Creditor, and Creditor agrees to accept from Debtor in the form of an **Extended Payment Plan**, payments to satisfy the indebtedness described in Paragraph 1 above as follows:

_____Dollars (\$_____) by the 15th of each month beginning on

__/__/_ (date) and ending on   /___/__

Payment is to be mailed every month in the form of a Cashier's Check or Money Order to the Creditor at his business address to be received no later than the 15th of each month.

B. Default by Debtor

Time is declared to be of the essence in this agreement and if the Debtor should fail to make the payment as provided in this agreement, the Creditor is released forever from his/her/its/obligation to accept from Debtor the lesser sum of _____Dollars (\$__) and shall have no further obligations under this agreement.

C.   Satisfaction

On full payment by the Debtor to the Creditor of the payment provided in Paragraph 3 above, the original indebtedness of the Debtor to the Creditor as described in Paragraph 1 shall forever be cancelled and discharged.

_____ (date) _____ (date)
Creditor   debtor

_____   _____
Witness for Creditor   Witness for Debtor

<u>Sample Letter to Prospective Client on your Letterhead</u>

Dear _____:

In recent times it is more common than not to hear of companies either downsizing or closing their doors. Lawsuits and court appearances are at an all time high. Most businesses who want to stay in business have all good intentions of paying their debts in a timely manner, however, situation can come up where money owed just starts to "snowball" – this is stressful, overwhelming and frustrating to say the least!

We are an Independent Negotiating Firm that saves money for businesses who would otherwise find trying to negotiate with their debtors too costly and time consuming. We negotiate your debt OUT OF COURT and are able to reduce overdue accounts by 40-80%. If there is a cash flow problem, payment plans agreeable to both parties can be extended. We work with attorneys, collection agencies, and creditors.

Our fee is dependent on RESULTS: if *we don't produce, you don't pay!*

The court system is so overburdened with cases it can sometimes take many months or even years to settle a case. Our negotiation process typically takes from a couple of days to a couple of weeks in most situations.

<u>YOU HAVE NOTHING TO LOSE, with our NO RESULTS – NO FEE System</u>.

Debts don't go away…they can report negatively on your credit reports resulting in credit denials limiting your purchasing power and the ability to conduct business. A Creditor has the right take you to court which will result in filing fees, legal fees and time lost whether you win or lose the case!

We are the Alternative to the Legal System!

If you would like to learn more about our Service, just give us 15 minutes of your time and let us confidentially show you how we can help you get back on track.

The consultation is FREE!

NOW YOU'RE ON YOUR WAY!

AFTER YOU CONDUCT A FEW RESOLUTIONS, YOU WILL REALIZE HOW SIMPLE THIS BUSINESS IS.

This book will lead you through a simple, guided process to owning and operating your successful and lucrative business in the field of

"BUSINESS TO BUSINESS DEBT NEGOTIATION'"

This exciting career brings with it much prestige and satisfaction.

Read these pages over and over again, study the forms, do your due diligence and most important:

ALWAYS PUT YOUR CLIENT FIRST!

"A meat and potatoes guide to starting your own Arbitration Business with almost no upfront costs! I've been looking for something like this for the longest time!" L.C. Atlanta, GA

"Don't let the size of this manual fool you! It is full of facts and clearly outlines how to run and grow this business" C. D. Staten Island, NY

"By following the steps laid out in this book, anyone with some drive and determination can own and operate a successful Debt Negotiating Business"
M.C., Cleveland Ohio

You don't need a degree or an elaborate education to do this! You can set it up fast, and start making money right away!"
O.S., Marietta, GA